18 Smart Ways to Improve Your Trading

Maria Psarra

Copyright © 2016 Maria Psarra
All rights reserved.
ISBN: 1908756810
ISBN-13: 978-1908756817 (ADVFN Books)

ADVFN BOOKS

Dedication

To Charles for making me see the whole picture, to my family for being by my side always, and to all those that said I'd never make it. Thank you.

Maria Psarra

Contents

Introduction	1
About the 18 Smart Ways	2
Chapter 1. How to Use Stop Loss Orders Effectively	3
Chapter 2. Protecting Profits	6
Chapter 3. Position Sizing	9
Chapter 4. Overtrading	12
Chapter 5. Being Afraid to Pull the Trigger	15
Chapter 6. Arrogance IS a Sin	18
Chapter 7. Refusing to Crystallise Losses	21
Chapter 8. Maria's Golden Rules for Trading CFDs: Part 1	24
Chapter 9. Maria's Golden Rules for Trading CFDs: Part 2	28
Chapter 10. Looking for the Holy Grail	32
Chapter 11. Summer in the Markets: Is It Worth It?	36
Chapter 12. Which Markets are Right for You?	41
Chapter 13. Size Does Matter	44
Chapter 14. Learning to Live with Uncertainty	48
Chapter 15. Staying Flexible	51
Chapter 16. New Beginnings	54
Chapter 17. What Now?	58
Chapter 18. Building Long-term Wealth with Dividend Income	62
Conclusion	65
About the Author	66
More books from ADVFN	68

Introduction

I never read book introductions, so I have decided not to really write one to my book either. I guess I am the type of person that does not enjoy spending much time on niceties. I like reality, facts, and cutting to the chase. So I will do just that.

This book is based on a series of articles I wrote for the Spreadbet and Master Investor Magazines over a period of a few years. The reason I wrote these, and my reason for publishing this book, is a promise I made to myself many years ago when I was a beginning trader. The promise was that when I got to the point where I had enough knowledge and experience to consistently make money in the markets, I would share this with other traders to help them in their own journey. When the time came, I delivered on my promise.

Trading has been a wonderful journey. I grew up through it, and I am incredibly grateful for this. However, even though trading will always be a huge part of me and my love for the financial markets will never change, I have come to see the whole picture, which is that trading is only a part of one's life. Now don't get me wrong, it is an amazing part, but a part nevertheless. These days, I choose to look at the whole of my clients' lives and my own. This whole encompasses a lot more than trading. It involves long-term investing, a truly holistic approach to wealth management, as well as inter-generational wealth accumulation and preservation. It encompasses every part of one's life and lasts forever, but this is a different subject that we will discuss in a future book.

For now, just remember that every trade ends, but we do not. We learn, evolve and become the best we can be. And we never ever stop. I do not anyway, and if you are reading my book, I believe you will not either.

I hope you enjoy my book.

About the 18 Smart Ways

This book contains explanations of the best habits of winning traders and investors, the most common mistakes the lack of these habits causes, and practical ways to avoid those errors.

Having spent the best of my last decade in the markets, trading for institutional proprietary trading desks and for myself, and advising and trading for mainly retail and professional clients, I have come across trading mistakes all too many times. I have made them myself, and have watched other traders and investors make each one of them as well. It is through this experience that I have learnt what the habits are that separate winning traders from losing ones, the secrets to profitable trading, and how to deal with the emotional hiccups that cause you to lose in the markets. It is exactly this knowledge that I want to share with you.

Before we go any further, I want to make you all aware of the fact that any trader or investor that tells you they have never lost money in the markets is too young, too stupid, too inexperienced, or just lying to you, and most often, they are really a combination of all of the above.

I hope that you will enjoy reading the book, and that it will make you a better investor or trader. I look forward to your feedback, and… happy trading, everyone!

The views expressed in this book are the author's personal views, not a representation of those of her employers. They are provided for information purposes only and in no way constitute advice.

Chapter 1
How to Use Stop Loss Orders Effectively

Winning traders set their stop losses based on a proven successful system designed to both protect them, and allow them to select suitable trades and profit from the markets. Losing traders on the other hand, set their stop losses based on randomly selected price levels and random potential percentage losses and monetary amounts, as well as based on the fear of losing any money trading, and the hope that all things in the markets, including this particular trade, will work in their favour.

Let's look into this in more detail. Winning traders always select trades that suit their broader macro view of the markets, their view of a specific security (whether this is a stock, an index or a different asset class) their timeframe (time they are willing to stay with a trading position) and their personal risk tolerance.

So how do winning traders really select their stop loss levels in practice? It is easier to illustrate this through an example.

Let's assume that the trader's macro view of the UK stock market is bullish; that is, the trader expects that UK stock prices will continue rising, and he wants to take advantage of this uptrend continuation by buying into individual UK stocks in the FTSE 100 and 250. Now his broader asset universe has been determined, the trader proceeds with selecting the stock/stocks he will buy. In order to do so the trader looks for a combination of fundamental and technical characteristics in a stock. Starting with the fundamental side, he wants to buy into a company with a healthy balance sheet and good future profitability prospects. He realises that it is important to know the company's past, so as to understand why the stock price is at its current level, and be able to make out whether the company's future is bound to be profitable or not, so as to decide on whether to buy into this future. So let us assume for our example that the trader has looked into company X, understands the past events that have brought the share price to its current levels, and believes based on his research that the company's future will be bright, so from a fundamental viewpoint, he is happy to buy it.

Now the trader determines the price levels that he would be willing to buy this stock at. This is where technical analysis comes in. The trader looks at the stock's chart (I use a daily chart for this purpose) in order to determine support/resistance levels for the stock. Winning traders always buy against a support level, and place their stop loss for the trade accordingly. So let's assume that the particular stock in our example has a support level at 100p, is currently trading above this, and moving higher. When buying a stock, winning traders want to risk as little as possible, only risk an amount that will not endanger their whole trading account, and what is more, risk an amount that if lost, will not prevent them from continuing to trade and look to make money in subsequent investments. Winning traders know that in the markets, same as in life, there will be times when they will fall and lose, so they make sure that when this happens, they have the strength and in the case of trading the financial ability, to get up and fight another day.

So let's assume for our example that the monetary amount that ticks all of the aforementioned boxes is £1,000. This translates into a maximum 10% stop for a £10,000 position in the stock, a 5% stop for a £20,000 position, and so on and so forth. This is the maximum amount the trader is willing to risk, and it is non-negotiable.

Now all of these have been determined, the trader looks at the price the stock is currently trading at, wanting to buy £20,000 worth of shares with a maximum monetary risk of £1,000, so a 5% stop. Winning traders will only buy into the stock if the current price fulfils all of their aforementioned requirements. If they do buy Stock X, their stop will be placed at a level just below the support level they are buying against, and if triggered will lead to a loss no greater than the maximum £1,000 that they are willing to risk on this trade.

If the price is not right in this way, winning traders will do nothing. They will add the stock to their watch list, and wait to buy in when and if the stock price comes to the right level in the future. They will not just pull the trigger and buy the stock regardless. By contrast, losing traders will just jump in, buy a randomly selected amount at the current market price, use a randomly selected stop, and hope for the best.

Well, as an old market saying goes, "There are old traders, and there are bold traders, but there are no old bold traders". The markets are not a charitable or forgiving place, quite the opposite, and any trader or investor believing that they can make and keep money in the markets over time based on their hope for the best, and as such on pure lack and inadequate risk management, will just never see their dream come true. This may sound harsh, but the markets are only going to be as harsh to you, the individual trader/investor, as you allow them to be, and on the other side of your every trade there is likely to be a winning trader, who among other things, will set their own stops in the way that makes them the winner.

So to summarise, next time you decide how to set your stop loss order for a trade, start by determining whether this is the right trade for you to begin with. This implies that it is your personal risk tolerance among other things that determines whether a trade is suitable for you, and not your wish to trade a particular security regardless of its suitability for you and your trading system at its current price levels. If the trade is indeed suitable for you, set your stop loss against the support/resistance level you wish to trade against, and just go for it. In any other case, you are much better off going for a walk, and either keeping the money you would risk in this trade for your future investing, or if you find yourself unable to do this, spend your money on something different that is guaranteed to entertain you, or give it all to a charity.

Chapter 2
Protecting Profits

I have heard this too many times from both investors and other traders: "I was making so much money in a trade, but then the market turned against me, and I ended up exiting the position making very little or even at a loss." Now I am no saint, I have sinned myself in this way many times as a novice trader, and then spent hours and days cursing and pitying myself about "What would have happened if…". However, I learnt from it. I saw what winning traders do differently and over time started doing the same myself. Hopefully after reading this chapter, you will have learnt a bit about how you can do things differently too.

So here goes, illustrated through an example.

You have made a good trade, and you are now looking at a healthy profit. Let us assume that you are holding £10,000 worth of company X stock, and are already 5% up on this trade. Today, following the announcement of the company's way above analyst consensus expectations half year results, the stock rallies by 15%, and as follows, you are now looking at a 20% profit, translating into £2,000. Not bad. Now what?

You tell your partner, your friends, your colleagues, jump happily up and down, and leave it at that. After all, you are such a good trader/investor, your trade selection is immaculate, and the company only reported today. So what could ever go wrong tomorrow morning?

The new day dawns, and around 9.30 am, the news hits the market. The company's CEO has "voluntarily" resigned as he has just been formally accused of repeatedly bribing foreign government officials in order to ensure their favourable treatment of the company's environmentally harmful activities in their country. The stock price has plummeted by 20%, and you, the "savvy" investor, have now lost yesterday's 20% profit.

You curse the departing CEO, the company, the institutional investors that sold their stock holdings early (as they surely "knew" long before you did), and think of how great it would have been if only you had cashed in your profits yesterday. Sounds familiar?

Well, we have all done it at some point, and suffered the consequences. In short, losing traders and investors rejoice in their success, appraise themselves and their ego for their exceptional trade selection abilities and stop exactly at this point.

Now what do winning traders and investors do differently?

It is simple. They protect their profits. How? They move their stops higher in order to "lock in" the profits from successful trades. In our example, they bring their stop up to lock in at least 10% of the total 20% profit they were making on the day of the company's results. This way, they end up exiting the trade next morning with a 10% profit.

They do not assume that what is here today will be here tomorrow. They do not believe that they are owed anything by the market because they are great traders. On the contrary, they thank the market and themselves for their existing profits, and ensure they keep them. They take what the market gives them, then walk away looking to make money elsewhere.

As we conclude this chapter, and you return to your trading, try to remember that "what the market gives, the market takes away", and the only person responsible for protecting your profits is you. The market does not owe you anything same as you do not owe anything to the market. Winning traders understand this, and ensure that when they have a profitable trade, no matter what happens from that moment on, they walk away making money. Winning traders understand that the reason for being involved in the markets is making money, not deriving excitement, boosting their ego, or proving to the world what amazing traders they are. This, however, is a subject, or rather a number of subjects, that we will discuss in more detail in the following chapters. For now, just remember that "the trend is your friend until the trend ends", and that moving your stops to protect profits ensures that you will be "out" when it does end.

As a famous trader once said, "You do need to make all the profit you could make from any one trade in order to make money in the markets. You just need to make more money than you lose over a number of trades and over time". So do not let your winning trades turn into losing ones. The truth is that you do not need to be "perfect" to make money in the markets, you just need to follow simple rules allowing you to be better than the millions of losing traders and investors around you.

Chapter 3
Position Sizing

Now ladies and gents, the time has come to talk about size, and in the markets size DOES matter. What does this mean? It means that it is not enough to find the right trade, and the right stop loss and profit targets for it, you also need to determine the right position size for this particular trade. So let's get quickly to the point, and as with the previous chapters, illustrate this with an example.

You have done your research, and identified Stock X, which appears to be a fantastic Buy according to your trading system's fundamental and technical selection criteria, and what is more, the stock it is currently trading just above its 52-week support level, and you, the savvy trader/investor have easily determined both your acceptable stop loss and first profit target levels. "Hurray!" you shout. "Trading comes so easily to me these days!" and continue, "This is TOO easy, I am TOO good. All that's left is to decide on one more minor detail, and I can jump in." Now in case you have not realised this by now, and I trust that many of you have, this final detail that is "minor" in your eyes, but not so "minor" in reality, is the actual size of the trading position that you will enter, or if you are a medium/long-term investor, the actual value of the investment that you will make.

At this point, most traders and investors will take the quick and easy road of arbitrarily choosing a position size that it is either too big or too small given the total size of their trading account. Following this, strangely more often than not, the two following alternative scenarios will unfold.

Scenario 1

The stock soon rallies thanks to unexpected good company news turning this into your most successful trade ever. That is the most successful in percentage terms, but, and here is the catch, due to the small position you took, sadly nowhere near interesting enough in monetary terms.

Scenario 2

The stock soon sinks due to unexpected bad company news. As any experienced trader/investor knows such things do happen in the markets, and are hardly the end of the world. That is unless you are the proud owner of a "too big to fail" position in this stock. "Too big to fail" in the sense that if it does, it will have an extremely big adverse impact on the value of your total trading account, your freedom to maintain your other existing positions, and even your overall ability to continue in the markets.

In either case, the result is far from great, and certainly not one that you or any market participant should aim for.

Obviously, less dramatic scenarios can occur as well, but for our example, I chose the two opposite ends of the spectrum in order to amplify and illustrate my point.

Now what do winning traders and investors do differently?

It is simple. They choose the right position size for their trades. How? Above all, they select a trade size that best matches the size of their personal trading account/investment portfolio. This briefly is a size that if the trade is proved successful will produce a sufficient return to justify the risk taken and boost their trading account, and on the contrary, if the trade turns unsuccessful, will cause no irreparable damage. Additional factors taken into account when determining trade size include personal attitude to risk, broader trading strategy, preferred investment time horizon, number and size of existing open positions in the portfolio, and in the case of fully invested leveraged portfolios, the ability to add additional funds to the account should adverse market movements deem it necessary.

In other words, winning traders ensure that their winning trades reward them well, and can always afford to best plan and execute this because they forbid their unsuccessful trades from causing any real harm to their account. Winning traders realise that their success in the markets does not depend on any single trade, and as such do not over-expose themselves by taking unsuitably large positions. On the flip side of this, they do not waste their time and effort by taking unsuitably small positions because they are afraid or unsure of the outcome. In summary, winning traders realise that no single trade should be allowed to make them or break them, and position size accordingly.

I certainly hope that after reading this chapter, you realise and accept this too. So next time you decide on the position size for your trades, remember to pick a size that is both worth your while if it succeeds, and allows you to fight another day if it does fail. Finally, always remember that picking more right than wrong trades over time, and managing them properly, will make you, as well as that one wrong trade, if unacceptably big enough, can and WILL break you.

Chapter 4
Overtrading

The next few chapters will look into the most common problems losing traders face: their emotional "roots", and how winning traders have dealt with them already. So let's start with two common bad habits, overtrading in this chapter and being afraid to pull the trigger in the next.

You may think that these are two opposite things, and in many ways, they are. However in reality, their cause is the same. This cause is usually the need to prove one's self right, and to avoid being wrong.

Let's start with overtrading. This is trading more often than one's trading strategy dictates, and as follows for no real reason. In other words, it means being excessively trigger-happy. We have all done this as beginning traders. We got carried away by our excitement for trading, jumped the gun, and more often than not got ourselves in rather messy situations as a result. Now, I have mentioned this before, deriving excitement is not a valid reason for entering the markets; looking to make money is. Trigger-happy traders look for excitement and leave trading results to luck.

In fact, they do not even think about the results, or about how they will manage the new trade, including their exit strategy, until after they have entered it. Before this, they only do one thing. I will let you guess which one… you are right, they are excited.

Let me give a few typical examples of this, which I believe will hit home. You are sitting in front of your PC one morning just before the UK market open, FTSE 100 constituent company X has just announced their way above analyst expectations annual results, and as soon as the stock opens for trading on the LSE, you realise that it has opened with a 10% gap above yesterday's closing price.

"Oh, if only I had bought a £10,000 worth position yesterday," you think, "now I would be £1,000 in profit". Correct, you could, and you would, but hindsight has never paid anyone. Winning traders realize this, and either would have taken the increased risk of buying into the company's results yesterday if they expected them to be this good, or if they haven't already bought in, will not jump the gun at this very moment buying at the current market price. If they are to buy into the stock following the 10% price rise at the open, they will do so at a later point (and not necessarily today) when the price has pulled back and they can get a better entry.

But not you, you just hate "seeing the market running away from you" and another "fantastic" opportunity to make money "like all the others are". So, you just pull the trigger, and buy the market... now. Needless to say, more often than not, you are now the proud owner of the stock bought at what will be proved to be the highest price of today's (and in some cases even following days') trading session. In other words you bought the high of the market. Everyone else had either already bought, or is waiting to buy after a pullback.

Now take into account that on a busy morning, when many FTSE 100 companies are reporting, you may get the rare opportunity to make similar trades five or six times, buying the absolute high of stocks that have gapped higher, and selling the absolute low of stocks that have gapped lower on their results at market open, all in the first 10-15 minutes of the trading session. You know you can be quick. You just execute the trades, you can always look at their results and pity yourself later.

Add to the above all of those times that you saw the price of any stock in companies not having just reported rallying higher, or crashing lower without you being on the profit train, and feeling left behind, and when you just jumped in without thinking, paying the then current market price, only to watch it immediately go against you afterwards, and you get the picture.

Now, I am sure you understand that leaving one's success on pure lack – which is exactly what you have done in all of the aforementioned examples – does not carry a huge probability of success in any area of life. The financial markets are no different. On the contrary, trading on luck guarantees failure in the not so distant future. Luck does not last long in the markets.

Each time we make a trade, we take on the inherent risk associated with it. The difference is that when we follow a proven strategy, this risk is calculated and of an acceptable level. In this way, we protect ourselves, and the value of our portfolio/trading account. Winning traders understand this. This allows them to go through the years making consistent money from the markets. Losing traders on the other hand do not. So next time you *feel* this sudden urge to pull the trigger for no valid reason, just do not do it. It is that simple. Emotions have no place in trading, and this is that simple as well.

We shall continue the next chapter with "Being afraid to pull the trigger".

Chapter 5
Being Afraid to Pull the Trigger

Now who is afraid of the big bad market? The truth is at some point we all have been, especially when we had just started trading, and had good reason to be so. We were too inexperienced to understand the markets, and/or we had made too many mistakes including the overtrading discussed in the previous chapter, to trust that our next trade would be profitable. We had been hurt too much, and as such we are now unwilling to risk experiencing any potential new pain by actually… trading!

Now let us not confuse being afraid to pull the trigger when our trading strategy dictates so, with feeling uncomfortable with the prevailing market environment in times where greater economic and political reasons lead to increased volatility and uncertainty of market direction. The latter is a valid reason for decreasing our exposure, or even staying out of the markets if necessary in order to protect the value of our portfolio until things settle. As with the previous chapters, this is best illustrated through an example.

The New Year has started, and you have made your 2015 commitment to only make trades that are dictated by your trading strategy. This year is going to be different, you ARE going to follow your rules, you will not repeat the same mistakes, you will not jump the gun for no reason, you will not hurt yourself and the value of your trading account/portfolio. This year WILL be different. That's what you keep repeating to yourself anyway.

So there you are sitting in front of your computer, having just completed your fundamental and technical analysis of Stock X, which according to every single one of your trading rules is a brilliant value Buy for you. To make things even better, the price level the stock is currently trading at is just right above support, you can place a stop perfectly suitable to your personal risk profile, and there is more than enough volume traded to fill your order easily at market.

All you have to do now is to enter the trade, pull the trigger. Simple as that. But what do you find yourself doing instead? You just sit there unable to move because you recall all those bad moments when you entered a trade (against your system's and really any reasonable system's or individual's argument that you should not), and shortly after, you lost money, and that hurt. And you do NOT want to feel that pain again. So you just stay there doing nothing instead. If you do not trade, you do not get hurt, right? You are absolutely right. If you do not trade, you risk nothing. The problem is you have no chance of winning anything either.

I often say that trading is very similar to real life, so I like using real life metaphors. In this light, what just happened to you in our example is the trading equivalent of the life situation where you are too afraid to date anyone, regardless of how promising they may be, because someone else broke your heart in the past. So it appears that the only solution for you to avoid future pain is to never get involved with anyone new moving forward. Correct? Now I really hope that you are laughing as you read this, because you understand how silly doing what I just described is. It is exactly as silly as not executing the trade in our example. So let's go back to trading.

I have mentioned this one before: the markets will only hurt a trader as much as the trader allows them to. In this sense, it is never about the market, it is all and always about the trader.

So what do winning traders and investors do differently? They follow a proven trading strategy, only take trades that are indicated by it, they leave their emotions out of trading, and they fully realize that when entering the markets they only have two goals, to make money, and to best protect themselves from… themselves, not the markets. Yes, they have lost money in trades, they have made mistakes, and same as you there was a time when they did not trust themselves enough to pull the trigger. But they got over it, they grew bigger and better, and so can you. There is no point in you being in the markets if this makes you suffer in any way. Again similarly to real life, if something hurts you, you do your best to fix it; if you succeed you stay, if not, you move on. That is all. This is exactly what you should do with your trading. That is, either change your approach and reactions to the markets, or just stay out of them for good.

Now most of you do not know me personally, but you can take my word that I am not fearless in personal situations, I have my "daemons", but I have no fear when it comes to trading my system and pulling the trigger. And if I was able to teach myself how to do this, hopefully so can you!

Chapter 6
Arrogance IS a Sin

Now ladies and gentlemen, this chapter is by no means religion-related, or about to discuss "Sin" in any even moderately religious context. I am only here to discuss the markets, and hopefully help you learn and improve from my past trading "Sins" and yours. So let's get on with it.

In this chapter we are looking at Arrogance, and how this can kill any trader or investor suffering from it.

Now, let me start by saying that I started my trading career at what was then one of the City's biggest proprietary trading desks, and had the luck to sit next to and learn from some of this world's best prop traders. I also had the unfortunate privilege of watching even the best of the best losing one too many millions for themselves and investors just because, amongst other things, they became too complacent, too convinced they were right, too arrogant.

Let me paint the picture for you. Back in those days, when one of us lost too much on any given trading position, our risk managers would come out of their own office, stand next to us at the trading desk, and ask us to close our positions. What do you think happened next?

Scenario 1

The trader closed their losing position as requested.

Scenario 2

The trader refused to listen, expressing his or her wrong arrogant views in a not so kind way, the house's position was closed by the Risk Managers, and the trader was escorted out of the office with the command not to bother returning until he or she could trade reasonably.

Scenario 2 occurred in the vast majority of cases. Let me add to this that back then, after a few years of successful trading, a prop trader would add his/her own funds on top of what the company and its institutional investors were entrusting him/her with, and in the cases where the trader was too arrogant to exit their position, Risk Managers would only close out the part of the position that corresponded to the company's and investors' holdings, whilst leaving the trader's personal percentage of them still running. In other words, they would let any of us traders blow ourselves up, so that we, and ONLY we could feel the pain. To this day, I thank them for doing this to me and the traders around me, because it taught me, among other things, that in the markets "Arrogance IS a Sin", and those that refuse to believe this will have to learn it the very hard way.

So… enough with my trip down memory lane, ladies and gentlemen. Let's talk about you… and let's do look at the uncomfortable truth.

Whatever you may think about yourself and your trading abilities, you are NOT God. Please feel free to substitute the world "God" with whichever higher power you believe in, so long as… it is NOT yourself. I am not preaching any religion whatsoever, just trying to bring home the message that the markets are bigger than you, me, or any individual trader or even institution, and as follows anyone being arrogant enough to claim that they are never wrong is really beyond joke territory, or as psychiatrists like calling this condition, suffering from delusion of grandeur.

Well, luckily for UK investors, the Financial Conduct Authority (FCA) prevents any regulated company or individual from promising potential and existing investors that they can deliver a performance that is 100% right. It follows that you should not deal with or trust anyone promising they can deliver this.

Equally importantly though, as many of you trade and invest for yourselves, you should not trust yourself to deliver such a thing either. Instead you should only trust those that say AND prove that they can deliver a realistically good trading performance. Without wishing to go into too much detail in terms of numbers in this chapter, this is those people that can consistently, over a period of time, pick many more winning than losing trades, risk manage both in such a way that guarantees trading accounts are up in the end of the chosen time period, whether this is six months, one year, five years or more, always depending on your own and their investment horizon. This is also those, whether that is you managing your investments or someone else advising you on them, that do not ridiculously overpromise. Instead… they simply deliver.

Actions and as such real trading performance, good risk management, AND lack of arrogance speak for themselves, ladies and gentlemen. They ARE by default louder than anyone's words. The rest, we are all better off and most likely richer living without.

Chapter 7
Refusing to Crystallise Losses

In this chapter we are looking at refusing to crystallize trading losses, the irreparable damage this can cause to your trading account (let alone to your soul) and how you can avoid this.

This subject is actually related to two of the previous chapters, namely *How to Set Stop Loss Orders Efficiently* and *Arrogance IS a Sin*. Let's explore how.

As I hope all of you realize, when one trades or invests, one should always accept the risk of incurring losses. Not every trade will be a winning trade, some trades are going to be unsuccessful, and they will come at a monetary cost. This, as any successful trader can testify, is just part of the game, and has not killed them in monetary terms or otherwise.

What, then, is this "Refusing to Crystallise Losses" problem?

Well, I otherwise call it the "It WILL come back" syndrome. This is the belief that any losing trading position or any losing medium/long-term investment you currently hold will eventually turn into a winning one. It may be down now, but if you hold on to it for long enough, and take enough pain watching it staying against you, you will eventually be proved right, it will make you money… eventually.

Now I am not here to dispute the basis of the theory of mean reversion. As you may know, according to it, financial assets like bonds or stocks tend to trade within a price range for relatively long periods of time, and as such, do eventually return to the mean.

There are a few problems with taking the above assumption too much to heart though, at least for individual investors and within reasonable timeframes.

Problem 1

Financial assets do NOT always mean revert within a reasonable period of time. Take for example the German Government 10 year Bonds (German Bunds). As many of you know, a bond's yield moves inversely to its price. In simple terms, when a bond's yield is falling, its price is rising, and vice versa.

The 10-year German bond yield has been falling since 2008 (late 2007 to an extent). All this time, its price has been rising. Not in a straight line, as nothing moves in a straight line up or down in the markets, nevertheless indisputably in this case, the price has been moving up for the last eight years now.

This means that you could have shorted the ten year Government Bond (or as would be the case its related Futures) at any point over the last seven years, and still be waiting in vain for its rising price to come back down to your entry. As you can see, to this day, it has NOT reverted back to its pre-2008 levels. Of course, it may do... eventually, but it is rather unlikely that even if you had the financial resources of a large institution, you could or should have stayed with this trade, refusing to just take your loss over the years.

Just to spice things up a bit, let me add a short personal story. There was a time when I used to trade German bond futures of different maturities. I will not bore you with the specifics of how I used to trade them, but will confess that I was sometimes too creative" Unfortunately, this led to my finding myself short a considerable amount of German Bund Futures on the morning that Ireland asked the European Union for a bailout, and guess what? The Bund Futures rallied.

Now, I could have waited to this day for the price to come back to my entry, but ladies and gentlemen, I can ensure you that it would have been in vain. Luckily, instead I just took a loss on that same day, and moved on. And this is exactly what you should do too when a trade really does not work.

Problem 2

Any financial asset can take longer to come back (assuming it one day does) than you can stay liquid for. You may have heard the saying that "the markets can remain irrational for longer than you can stay solvent". It IS true. So even if you are going to become right as a product of holding your current lossmaking positions into the future, there is a huge probability that after some point, you will no longer be liquid enough to hold on to anything.

Problem 3

Even if you are liquid enough to hold on to bad positions for prolonged periods of time, doing so is definitely not the best use of your available trading capital. No one has unlimited resources. So why waste yours by tying up your money in lossmaking positions? You are much better off crystallizing your losses at the right time, and using your capital in order to make money elsewhere.

Problem 4

Some financial assets never come back to the price you bought them. A good example of this is the stocks of junior oil explorers. Some of these companies never discover oil, at least not enough, and one day, well, go bankrupt.

So to conclude, next time you refuse to crystallize a loss despite your trading system's clear indication that you should, do please try to remember the above, and ask yourself if the real reason that you refuse to take this loss is just protecting your ego. If it is, may I please remind you that the markets hardly ever stay merciful for long enough with any trader or investor that does not control his/her ego.

Chapter 8
Maria's Golden Rules for Trading CFDs: Part 1

Ladies and gentlemen, I do realize that we were just beginning to touch upon the subject of "Deadly Trading Sins" in the last few chapters, so I really hope that you will forgive me for changing the subject for this and the next one following the recommendation of my friend and renowned City Market Strategist, Zak Mir, in light of our Traders' Panel Discussion during the 2016 London Master Investor Show.

We shall continue our trip down the "Sins" lane in later chapters (and mind you, I am no saint, I just know how to keep my sins out of my Trading, and hopefully one day you will too). So for now, let's just look at my Golden Rules for Trading CFDs.

Rule 1 – Avoid Overleveraging

Do NOT overleverage your accounts ladies and gents. CFDs are one of the most flexible financial products ever invented, but they are also one of the riskiest ones. If you do not know how to play with fire, then just don't. If you do not trust yourself, but trust someone else enough, hire them to help you. If you do not know such a person either, stay away. And finally… if you think you are better than the professionals, then good luck, prove it, and I shall give you my own money, seriously.

So what do I mean by overleveraging? I start with the assumption that all the funds in your trading account are funds that you can afford to lose (and if not, then too bad, they shouldn't have been there in the first place), so the maximum of these funds that should ever be used for the total of your open positions is 80% at any given time. And this IS the maximum. The rest (at least 20% at any given time) should just sit there in cash. You are NOT God, I am not either, as such we cannot predict Lehman Brothers, MF Global, a plane crashing on the Tower of London, the End of the World As We Know It. You just have to accept that remote as the probability of such an event happening may appear to be, it is definitely not zero. I have. I guess watching Lehman Brothers fail, and having my money tied up in MF's liquidation, helped to open up my doors of perception. So, coming back to you and to today, if a similar Black Swan event happens, you want that minimum 20% of remaining capital discussed to get you through the next and rainy days.

Rule 2 – Position Sizing

We discussed this one in a recent chapter, and as I believe I have repeatedly mentioned before, in the markets, size DOES matter. In short, too big can kill you every time, and too small is just not worth your while. What is more, by some weird coincidence, you will find that you will always tend to lose money in the trades you went too big with, and win money in the trades you went too small with. So how about you just try to determine a suitable position size for each of your trades given the size of your trading account and risk tolerance, and adhere to it?

Rule 3 – Selecting Suitable Stop Loss Orders

Let me start by saying that I do not personally use stops when trading normal stocks. I also did not use stops when I used to trade Futures intraday discretionarily for myself and institutional clients. In both cases, the reason was the same. I could control the risk I was taking, and exit the position when necessary. Stocks are not leveraged, therefore for any liquid stock, the risk that you are carrying by buying it is 95% and below of the risk that you have by carrying the same monetary amount in a CFD position. Yes, you could bring the size down so that you have the same exposure, but let's be honest, this is not why CFDs were invented – they were invented to provide short-term leveraged exposure/profits to those that can achieve them. So if you are to ever receive the benefits of this, you have to learn to control the downside.

As for the Futures I used to trade, our way of trading at the time involved around 70 scalping trades per day; we had to be married to our trading screens, and react like an algorithm. These days are gone as any prop trader of that era will tell you, and such tasks are now best performed by real algorithms.

So that leaves us with the present, and with the fact that when trading CFDs, it is best to use trading stops. And as I discussed in one of the previous chapters, these stops should be placed at the price points where the market proves you wrong. For example, when you are long a stock CFD, this stop price is below the support level you bought it against.

Rule 4 – Be Flexible

Nobody likes being wrong. It hurts, and it always comes at a price. However, confident people are not afraid to be wrong. So when they make a decision, they are: 1. ready to fully support it without doubting it for no reason, and 2. happy to admit that this decision was either always wrong, or is no longer right if the conditions that led to it happen to change.

Let me give you an example. Back in May 2015, I was short Fresnillo, and was making money in the trade. Then, one evening, a US Fed announcement came out stating that interest rates may be raised earlier than expected. Following this, gold shot up. For me that meant that Fresnillo (being a FTSE 100 gold and silver miner) was also going to shoot up as soon as the UK stock market opened next morning. So I went to the office that morning, and advised all of our traders and clients to exit their related positions. Did we lose money in this? In some cases we did, yes. We for sure lost the profits we were making beforehand. And so what? The reason for being in this trade was no longer there, we were no longer right, so our only reasonable option was to exit. And that was OK. I can ensure you that taking the loss at that point made no big negative difference to anyone's weekly, let alone monthly P&L. I can also ensure you that staying short Fresnillo after this point would have.

This concludes the first part of my Golden Rules for Trading CFDs. We shall continue with the remaining six rules in the next chapter of this book.

Charter 9
Maria's Golden Rules for Trading CFDs: Part 2

This chapter continues with my Golden Rules for Trading CFDs.

Rule 5 – Have a Plan, and Stick To It

This is one of the most important rules of trading, and it remains the same regardless of whether you are trading CFDs or any other financial product. Every trader, every investor has different goals, different experience, different risk tolerance, and really a different life and personality. Your plan should be such that it is suitable for you personally having taken into account all of the aforementioned criteria. *"Wanting to make money quickly"* may be something I keep hearing from traders and investors over the years, but I can ensure you that it is in no way a viable trading plan. It is simply and only a wish.

Furthermore, it is not enough to have a plan, you also have to follow it. Otherwise, even the best plan in the world will have zero value to you.

Rule 6 – Select Markets and Financial Products that are Suitable for your Risk Tolerance, your Experience, and your Financial Situation

These products may or may not include CFDs. I do not have the right answer for you without knowing you, and discussing things with you in person. The FCA's "Assessing Suitability and Appropriateness" tests can help you and your advisors assess this one.

What I can and will say, however, is that you need to fully understand any financial product and the risks associated with it prior to trading it. No one was born with this type of knowledge, we all had to learn, we all asked stupid questions, and we all got things wrong when first approaching any new product. In fact, we all still do with products we have not traded before. So do please ask questions, clearly understand, and then choose that which is suitable for you.

Rule 7 – Only Risk Money you can Afford to Lose

This applies to any given moment in time and to any financial product you trade. It is even more so the case with derivatives products like CFDs, Futures, and Options, where you can lose more than your initial investment. To clarify, I am in no way implying that you should not trade derivatives products, I personally tend to prefer them to cash equities/bonds, as they are much more "flexible". I am only repeating the point made earlier which is that you should understand the products you trade, so that you can then assess whether specific trades, if made, will not make you risk more than you can afford to lose.

In reality, the point I am making is the same for any financial product, because I am actually making a point about you. That is that you have to find out what is the amount of funds that if lost, will realistically not make a change to your life (and by life I do NOT mean your ego, I mean things like your rent, your children's school fees, your retirement plans, etc). This amount is your risk capital, and this is the maximum and only capital that you should put at risk in the markets (and elsewhere if I may add).

Rule 8 – Keep Emotions Out of your Trading, and Even More So Out of your CFDs Trading

Why? Because to begin with, as we have discussed in the previous chapters, emotions simply do not have any place in trading and investing, so do keep them out of these. I can ensure you that although most of you will never witness this, I am rather emotional when it comes to my personal life, and yet I am not emotional when trading. I have trained myself to do this, and so can you.

Now why "even more so out of your CFDs' trading"? Simply because when you trade CFDs, your exposure to the asset you are trading is magnified, so you may as well not magnify any loss of control issues you have through it. You are better off ensuring you can control yourself first, before trading anything, including CFDs.

Rule 9 – Use CFDs to Diversify

In other words, do not put all of your eggs in one basket. CFDs allow you to take the same exposure you otherwise would when, for example, buying physical shares in a company by putting down just a small initial deposit (otherwise called margin). So do use the remaining funds in your trading account in order to buy/sell other stocks, commodities, or whatever better suits your goal to profit from the prevailing market conditions.

Rule 10 – Protect Yourself, Use CFDs for Hedging When Necessary

Once again, CFDs are a flexible tool. They allow one to go long or short, and as such allow one to profit from both rising and falling asset prices. Take advantage of this flexibility. Nothing goes up or down in a straight line, so there are bound to be opportunities on both sides of the markets over any given period of time. Use them to make money.

Furthermore, if you are for example a long-term Equities investor, and you are scared that the Third World War may just be starting (imaginary scenario obviously), do use CFDs to protect yourself. How? Go short a related index, buy some "stress and fear antidotes" such as gold or Government Fixed Income CFDs just to name a few options.

Remember, the markets will only ever do to you what you allow them to, so whatever the situation is, just learn to use the right tools to protect yourself and the value of your trading account. CFDs are one of the best products to achieve this so long as… you use them wisely.

This concludes my Golden Rules for Trading CFDs.

Chapter 10
Looking for the Holy Grail

Now ladies and gentlemen, following the completion of "Maria's Golden Rules for Trading CFDs", it is time to continue with our educational chapters focussing on the best habits of winning traders and investors, the most common mistakes traders make and the best ways to avoid them.

Our subject for this chapter is the ever famous search for the Holy Grail in trading and the financial markets.

So what do I mean by Holy Grail? Please allow me to clarify. The Holy Grail is this one single trade whose successful conclusion will make you richer than your wildest dreams. It will produce a return of for example 300% in the space of a few days.

For example, you buy stock X today, it goes up by 300% by next week. Now don't get me wrong, I am not saying that this can never happen, up to a certain extent, it can, and it does. In fact, this is what often happens when a junior oil explorer discovers oil in one of their exploration fields, or when a junior miner secures permissions to explore a likely gold-rich geographic area of the world.

What I am saying, however, is that forever looking for, and investing all of your available funds in, this one junior explorer that if successful in their efforts will make you filthy rich is by no means a fool-proof trading strategy, nor is it a prudent way to achieve consistent returns over the years.

Obviously when saying this, I assume that one's investments involve no element of market manipulation, use of inside information or any other related form of financial crime that both me and the FCA would clearly advise you to abstain from.

You see, what I am about to share may sound a little mean, but I am convinced that there is a very specific reason that occasional financial press celebrities who claim they consistently make 300% returns in their trades in very short periods of time cannot "sell" to professional traders like me. This reason is that I have seen enough of the markets to realize that they are either lying, or are actually guilty of some form of market manipulation, insider trading, etc offence. In either case, I would rather keep as far away from this type of people and situations as possible.

I believe that trading and investing are a business, and should be approached as such. As some of you will know from running your own business, or simply ensuring that your daily work contributes towards your employer's success and revenue stream, businesses need to be consistently performing and profitable in order to survive and prosper. The exact same principles apply to investing and trading.

As any honest professional investor will tell you, the way to make money in the markets is to be consistently profitable over a period of time. This period is not a few months or years, rather it is many years or even a lifetime. In order to achieve this one needs many small winning and losing trades, a few big winners, and no big losers.

One is bound to have big winners over time, but not necessarily by design, or because one is focussed on this. Let me give you an example of this that I often come across in my own trading, and advising my clients. Many of my clients as well as myself like trading companies' annual or semi-annual results announcements, by buying into the company's stock a few days or even the previous day before the announcement when looking for good results, or alternatively selling short the company's stock when we believe the results are going to be bad.

One of the trades of this type I advised clients on, and discussed on TV, was a Buy in Workspace Group (WKP.L). The company reported its annual results on 6 March 2015, these greatly beat analyst expectations, and the stock closed 6.52% up on the day. In money terms, this means that if you had bought £10,000 worth of Workspace shares during the last days preceding the announcement, you would have made a profit of £652 at market close on 3 March. If you had used leverage, that is CFDs products, for this £10,000 trade, you would have made five times that given that the CFD's margin for Workspace is 20% with most UK clearing brokers, so a £10,000 initial deposit would have given you exposure to £50,000 worth of the underlying shares, so a gross profit of £3,260. This is a 32.6 % return to your initial investment in the space of a few days.

So yes, quick high returns ARE possible even in liquid FTSE 100 and FTSE 250 stocks. The point I made earlier though is that they are neither the actual trading strategy nor the Holy Grail. Rather they are the result of adopting a well-researched trading strategy. In this particular case, the strategy involves buying into companies that have been doing well, and selling short companies that have been doing badly prior to their results' announcements. Although making such trades obviously entails a higher level of risk than just buying and holding blue chip shares for the long-term, it is (or at least should be) based on thorough analysis of the company's past financial performance, competition, related news flow, and other factors. In other words, it involves taking a calculated risk, and is neither gambling, nor hoping and wishing for this one single trade that will make you rich. Furthermore, it is not every time a company reports good results, that you see its stock price rise by 6.5% on the day. Most times, even if results announcements are good, liquid stocks tend to move by a 1-2% higher instead, and you will have to learn to be happy about achieving these small winnings, because the truth of the matter is, that as long as you manage your risks properly, these will ensure you make consistent money over time.

I do repeat this to my clients and traders I train; the financial markets are NOT where you should derive all of your life's excitement from. Taking this one step further, the markets are also not a place where you should expect to win the lottery, or meet your one true love, the quest for both of which closely resembles investors' ongoing quest for the Holy Grail. Yes, you may get lucky enough to actually win the lottery, or meet your one true love on any day. After all, "Who am I to disagree" when as an old song goes, "I travelled the world and the seven seas, and everybody is looking for something," but just until you find either, how about you focus on consistently growing your trading capital in a more consistent way? Hopefully, after reading this chapter you are at least more open to the idea.

Chapter 11
Summer in the Markets:
Is It Worth It?

Is trading and investing during the summer really worth it? This is a question I hear from investors every single year anytime from May onwards. It is also a very popular argument in both investors' and professional traders' circles.

I am sure you are all familiar with the old adage, "Sell in May, and go away," but for many of you the question still remains, "Should I sell out of my entire portfolio in the beginning of summer, and only look to re-invest come next autumn?" Let's look at a bit of history first.

The "Sell in May, and go away" saying dates back to the old City of London "glorious" days, when stockbrokers took their summer vacation in May and did not return until September. Their time away was directly linked to the English race horse season, in which horse races begin in early June, with the final horse race of the season taking place on St Leger's Day in September. As stockbrokers were absent during this time, the market was illiquid and pretty flat. "Those were the days," I hear many of you saying upon reading this, and can assure you that there are times when I feel exactly the same, but to be fair, even though trading volumes tend to decrease over the summer, no stockbroker or trader is entitled to such long holidays anymore.

Furthermore, the financial products available to investors have greatly changed since this old City adage was invented, with more flexible products having become freely available to everyone, products providing both institutional and individual investors with opportunities to profit from both rising and falling markets in every major asset class. This means that even in the years when the stock markets do move lower between May and September, you can still make money by being short an index CFD or future.

July 2015 when this chapter was written is a good example of this. I have included here a chart of the FTSE 100 Index, where you can see that had you taken a short position using a FTSE CFD or Futures Contract at the 7,000 level last May, you would be up by 550 points when the index hit 6,450 following this. In monetary terms, assuming that you had used a CFD to take a £100 per point short position at 7,000 in May 2015, you would have a £5,500 gross profit when the index reached 6,450. So last year, the "Sell in May" theory worked on an overall market level. In fact, according to research, it has worked in most years since 1950 both for the FTSE 100 and the US Indices.

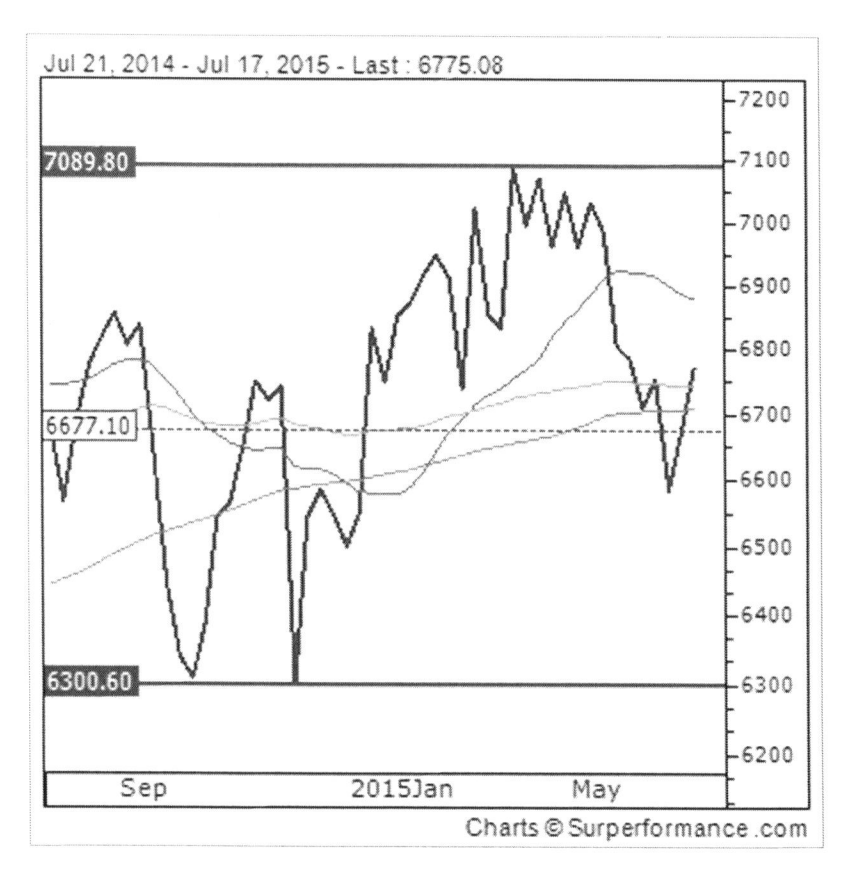

There is, however, a catch: the theory does not always work. The stock markets do not always go down in the summer, so it follows that profiting by simply "selling in May" is not a fool-proof strategy. To show this, I have included here a chart of the Nasdaq Index, where you can see that going short in May 2014, or alternatively selling out of all of your Nasdaq stocks, would have been the wrong thing to do. As seen on the chart, if you had shorted the Nasdaq at 3,550 that May, you would have been down by 450 points when it hit 4,000 in September 2014. Hopefully, if you were indeed short, you would have exited at a loss before then. Alternatively, if you had sold all of your Nasdaq stocks that May, you would probably be pretty angry with yourself come September.

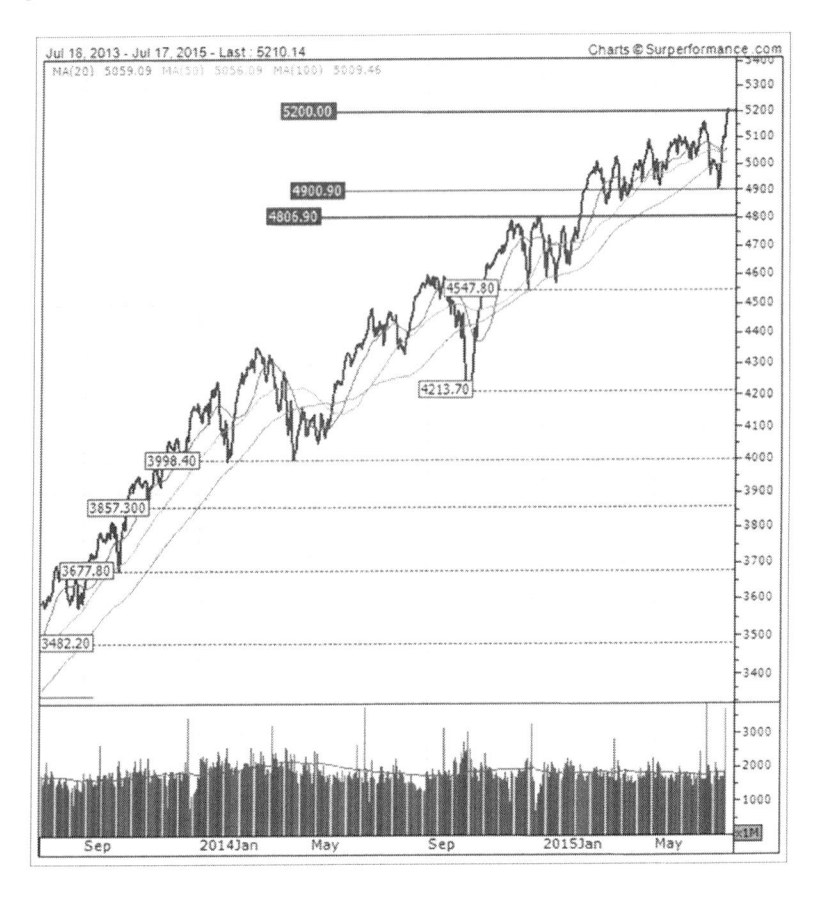

Having looked at all this, let us now focus on you. What should YOU do in the summers? Well for starters, you neither have to exit all of your stock positions in May, nor do you necessarily have to go short. As is always the case with the markets, you should base all of your investing and trading decisions on facts, reason, and correct assessment of the current market and greater economic environment. You should do this regardless of the season, not only in the summertime. If you do this right, you will know that there are Mays when you will be best off selling, and Mays when you will not, and then you will just have to act accordingly.

Since we are talking about you though, let's stay on this topic, and discuss when you should stay away from the markets in summer regardless of the markets' direction. Let's start with the basics. I hope you agree that you should only make investment decisions when you can think clearly. This is most unlikely to happen after you have had your third vodka cocktail under the sun on a Mediterranean or Caribbean beach. Just because trading technology and wireless internet provision have improved enough to allow you to trade from anywhere, anytime, it does not mean that you should do it. If there is a place and a time for everything in this life, the beach and your holidays in general are not the place and time for trading. So how about you do yourself a favour, and forget about the markets whilst you are away?

"But what about my existing open positions?" I hear some of you say. Well, it is simpler than you think. In fact, I can summarize it in the following two rules:

1. Close your highly leveraged (CFDs) positions before you go on holidays.

2. Ensure that all of your remaining open positions have protective stops in place. Use trailing stops if you wish to progressively lock in profits.

That IS the long and short of it ladies and gentlemen. It is not rocket science, it is just you applying the same exact principles that you should be applying all year round.

"Yes, but," I now hear the unconvinced among you ask, "What if a major disaster strikes? A new 9-11, a huge nuclear explosion, the Third World War, the End of the World?" Well, believe it or not, if a major disaster does happen, assuming that the markets do still exist and are open, and you have followed rules 1 and 2 above, you may hit your stops, you may have these filled at worse prices than you would otherwise, but you will not lose all of your money. It will NOT be the end of your trading/investing.

Now of course, if the major disaster was to be the start of the Third World War, may I suggest that you cut the holiday short, go home, sell your stocks at any price, and simply look for ways to protect yourself and your family thereon? And finally, if the major disaster really IS the End of the World, may I suggest that you stop caring about the markets altogether, and just enjoy your last moments? I know I will.

Hopefully, I have not scared you, or made you feel uncomfortable with my disaster discussion; instead I have succeeded in showing you a way to have a more relaxed and profitable summer this year.

Chapter 12
Which Markets are Right for You?

So which markets are really right for you, ladies and gentlemen? This is the topic of this chapter.

Now what do I mean by "which markets"? I mean is it Stocks, Bonds, Forex? If it is stocks, is it the large cap dividend aristocrats type, the AIM young, high risk, high potential reward plays? Both? Neither? And even after you have decided which of the aforementioned asset categories you prefer, what financial products should you use to gain exposure to them? Is it going to be cash Equities/Bonds, Futures, Options, CFDs, Spread Betting? And is it going to be the UK market? Europe? The US? Asia? Choices, choices, choices!

It's a whole wild world, and these days numerous options are available to you when it comes to how and what to trade and invest in the global financial markets. So how do you make your own personal choice? How do you find what is right for you?

Well, let us start with the basics. First of all, I am sure you will agree that whatever you decide to trade and invest in should be suited to your financial situation, attitude to risk, and level of financial knowledge. It should also suit your personality, your daily schedule, and the amount of time you can devote to researching, executing and monitoring your trades.

So let us first look at your financial situation. Prior to investing in anything, you need to determine the level of capital that is available to you for this purpose. When looking at the financial markets especially, this is an amount that if lost, will not negatively impact your lifestyle. Now, I am not saying or implying that you WILL indeed lose this money, I am however saying that you should be perfectly fine with accepting this possibility. Furthermore, any investment carries an inherent risk. As I am sure you will have heard before, the value of investments does fluctuate, and this is another reason why you should only use risk capital for your investments. There is no point in you risking your funds in even the best investment in the world today, if you may need to liquidate it tomorrow morning in order to pay your daughter's school fees. If this is the case, you should just not make the investment today. You should wait until you have more capital available.

For this chapter, we shall assume that you have determined your risk capital to be £100,000. Now you need to decide what sort of financial products (and in some cases services) are available to you. By default, some things like hedge funds, private equity, government bonds, etc are not available to you, as they require higher initial investments. So the investment universe is now a bit narrower.

The next thing you should consider is your financial experience. That is which markets have you been involved in before, and which financial products have you used for this purpose? For those of you that have worked in the financial services industry, this answer tends to be straightforward. However, for most individual investors, this is not the case. So even if you have never invested before, you need to ensure that you choose markets and products that you understand fully and clearly. For example, derivatives products like Options or CFDs are less straightforward than Cash Equities. So if you are only just beginning to invest, and are planning to do this without any professional training or advice, you are better off starting with "normal" stocks than with Options or CFDs on them. You can always move into using Derivatives in the future if you wish.

Continuing our example, we shall assume that you have decided that you are going to use your £100,000 in order to invest in UK stocks. You chose the UK market as you are more familiar with UK companies (in many cases you use their products or services), and want to be able to conduct all your trades over the course of normal

UK work hours. Also, if you are like most investors, you do not like the idea of your stocks continuing to move when you are asleep.

Now, you need to determine what sort of stocks are suitable for you. This primarily depends on two things, namely your attitude to risk, and your investment goal. Let me explain.

Starting with your attitude to risk, you must decide how much volatility you can stomach, not only financially, but also emotionally. As a rule of thumb, certain sectors of the stock market such as mining or the financials are more volatile. Also, the lower the trading volume of a stock, the more volatile it tends to be. As follows, FTSE 350 stocks tend to be much less volatile than those listed on the AIM market. So, assuming that you personally dislike too much movement, you should only invest in FTSE 350 stocks, or even just the blue-chip FTSE 100 ones.

Now your investment goal. Are you looking for income, capital growth, or even a combination of both? If the answer is income, you must focus on high dividend paying stocks. These tend to be the stocks of well-established, successful companies in defensive sectors. If, by contrast, you are just looking for capital growth, you should focus on more exciting, high-growth companies in non-defensive sectors, such as technology.

Having considered all these, we shall assume you have decided that you are looking for capital growth, and are happy to bear some volatility, but not enough to invest in AIM stocks. So now you know that your investment universe is FTSE 350 stocks with a focus on fast growing companies.

Finally, you need to decide how much time you can devote to your trading and investing on a daily and weekly basis, and build your trading strategy around it. Obviously, the more time you have available, the more frequent and shorter-term your trades can be. Just as with everything else we discussed in this chapter, this is for you to decide. I hope that this has made your future investment decisions more straightforward.

Chapter 13
Size Does Matter

Now ladies and gentlemen, I am sure you have heard (and perhaps even said) the expression "Size matters" many times in your life. I know I have. But before we get over-excited, and start thinking of potentially more amusing but certainly irrelevant matters, let me clarify that I am in this instance solely referring to the size of the companies whose stocks you invest in.

We discussed "Which Markets are Right for you" in the previous chapter. Today we shall take this one step further, and look at which stocks are right for you from an issuing company size perspective. What I mean by this is whether you should be focussing your investments on large caps, small caps, or both.

So how do you make your decision? Let us take a look at the things you should take into account.

1. Risk

This is your personal attitude to risk. In general, investing in large, long-established companies carries less risk than investing in their smaller, younger counterparts. When looking at the UK stock market, this means that investing in companies whose stocks are listed on the FTSE 350 carries less risk than investing in stocks listed on the AIM market. There are three main reasons for this. The first one is obvious in the sense that the longer and more successfully a business has operated for, the greater the likelihood that it will continue to do so. Yes, I hear some of you say, but even big UK banks like Lloyds almost failed during the last financial crisis. You are right. However, regardless of your opinion on government bailouts, you cannot possibly ignore the fact that at least these companies were important enough for the government to step in and provide a lifeline. It is unlikely that the UK government will ever step in to save a junior oil explorer instead.

The second reason why investing in FTSE 350 companies carries less risk is that these are more liquid, that is there are larger volumes traded in them on a daily basis. This makes these stocks less volatile – they tend to move less and are not so prone to sudden large price moves. Furthermore, liquid stocks are easy to trade in and out of for individual investors as there is enough available volume in the market to fulfil their buy or sell orders. This is often not the case in the AIM where one often has to ask brokers to work on filling one's order by sourcing liquidity from other investors and market makers, and where exactly because this is the case, one should be flexible with regards to the price and time required for orders to be filled.

The third reason is that the LSE's requirements for a company to list on the main market are stricter than those for the AIM. By requirements I mean both the capitalisation (market value of a company) and the level of detail and accuracy with which a company reports its financial performance. It is important to understand that what is missing from the additional reporting requirements increases the risk of investing in a company as there is a lot that an AIM-listed company does not have to disclose to the investing public.

Now, please do not regard the above as an attempt to discourage you from investing in the AIM market. It is not. I do advise clients on investing in AIM shares myself. The above is rather my attempt to make you correctly assess the risks inherent in investing in different types of stocks.

2. Income vs Capital Growth

Are you looking for dividend income, price appreciation (or alternatively depreciation when shorting a stock), or both? As a rule of thumb, companies that have been in operation for longer, and have been more profitable tend to pay higher dividends than those who have not. However, this is just a rule of thumb as a company's dividend policy ultimately rests with its management, and is based on several things, including the company's future expansion plans, which can divert cash away from dividend payments and into other things such as acquiring smaller rivals, building additional factories, etc. As follows, a lower dividend payout does not necessarily mean that a company is doing worse than one with a higher one. It does mean, however, that if looking for income, your money is better invested elsewhere.

Furthermore, when looking for income, it is important to assess how safe and stable the dividend is and may continue to be. I shall not go into details of how such checks are performed here, but please bear in mind that this is an important parameter to take into account.

To conclude, if you are indeed looking for dividend income, you should focus on investing in the dividend aristocrats of the FTSE 350 instead of in their AIM counterparts.

3. Investment Horizon

This is how long you wish to hold your investment for. In my view, one should have a longer term horizon when investing in AIM stocks. This is because often these are younger, higher growth companies that are looking to expand more than their large cap counterparts. As anyone that has ever worked for a "young" company, including myself, can testify, expansion tends to take more time than companies' management expects. So you should only invest in such companies if you have the patience and financial flexibility to stick around to see them grow and succeed.

4. Products that you Wish to Use for your Trading

The financial products you use for your trading and investing should be suited to your attitude to risk and your experience. In the case of individual UK stocks, your choices are Cash Equities, CFDs, and Options. I have deliberately left Spread Bets out of this discussion as they are not classified as a "financial product" by the FCA, and I do not advise clients on them.

The smaller a company is, the more unlikely you are to find CFDs or Options on its stock offered by clearing brokers. As follows, if your trading strategy is based on using such products, you must stick more with large cap stocks. Furthermore, when it comes to CFDs, you should be aware of the fact that not every UK-listed stock is shortable either due to regulatory restrictions, or due to clearing brokers' own limitations on the size of companies (and average daily traded volume of their stocks) on which they offer CFDs.

Personally, I have had enough arguments over the years about not being able to trade CFDs on certain stocks, but I have to respect the clearing brokers' argument, and so have you. Having said this, I tend to oppose the use of CFDs for investing in small AIM stocks as their volatility is already enough for my personal risk profile and trading systems. In general, I tend to think that when one is investing in AIM stocks one is better off just simply buying and holding.

Chapter 14
Learning to Live With Uncertainty

Accepting uncertainty, and learning to best live with it in your trading and investing, is the topic of the chapter. From now on we will focus more on the best habits of winning traders, and less on the mistakes traders and investors make. Even though, to be fair, these two are just like the two sides of a coin, same as the best and worst of everything in life tends to be.

So what do I mean by "Learning to live with uncertainty?" In this particular occasion, I mean that when it comes to trading and investing, you have to accept that you will never know the final outcome of any of your actions from the outset, and that if you wish to remain sane, sound and liquid, this is something you do have to accept and embrace.

I believe this is a timely discussion given the levels of volatility we have been experiencing in the world's financial markets these last months, and which in my view are going to persist for the near future. So what does this increased volatility and, as follows, uncertainty mean for you as an individual trader or investor?

Does it mean that you should do nothing? Stay on the side-lines? Not invest or trade? Well, if that is what makes you happy, then you actually should. But if it is not what you really want, then may I suggest that you learn to live and cope with your fear of uncertainty? Easier said than done, I hear you say, and I agree. Uncertainty is not an easy thing to live with... for anyone, including myself.

In fact, if my work colleagues could speak now, they would probably tell you that I have what appears in their eyes as an unnecessary fear of crossing the street at the wrong time for fear of being killed by a car. Somehow, this is not an uncertainty I want to take on, so I prefer to wait until the green light hopefully makes it safe for pedestrians to cross.

However, I am most happy to trade and advise clients to trade using highly leveraged products when I feel the opportunity is suitable. I am also most happy to fall in love, trust certain people, start a new business, all of which can hardly be described as being risk-averse. So I cannot possibly pretend that I despise risk; I guess I do embrace it. And still... I want you to know that there is always a level of stress that goes with each one of my trades, or decisions, however smaller this may have become over the years.

My goal for this chapter is not to make you take more or less risk than is right for you, rather it is to help you understand what the right amount of risk for you may be. In the end, it is all about understanding yourself, and pursuing what makes you happy. So let us see if I can be of some assistance.

The way I look at it, both the long- and short-term have a place in our lives, and this applies to all of our investments, financial or otherwise. The point is, though, we have got to understand the difference between the two, so that we enter and exit our investments of any form at the right time. When it comes to the financial markets, we also have to understand the current environment, stay flexible, and go with the flow. We shall discuss staying flexible in a future chapter, but for now, it is enough to say that part of successfully living with uncertainty involves you changing sides in order to make more money, or avoid losing it.

Trading and investing is NOT about being always right, it is not even about being fundamentally right but letting this cost you money, it IS just about making money. Period. As follows, in an environment of increased volatility, you have to stay flexible.

Let me give you a real life example. One of my most successful trades for 2015 was to short Glencore shares. It worked wonderfully well, we made money, our clients were happy, but we also exited at the point, where we saw too much buying coming in and pushing the market higher. Staying in after that point whatever my view is of the company, would impose on us a level of uncertainty that I am not willing to bear. So we exited. Did I know that Glencore shares would find so much of first selling, then buying when we first entered the trade months ago? Of course not. I did however believe that based on our fundamental assessment the shares would move lower before we first went short, and that the market no longer saw enough reason to sell (rather to increasingly buy in) when we exited our shorts.

And more than this, do I know that every single trade I make is going to be right? No I don't. What I do know is that I have done my research, I am following my system, and based on these, I am willing to take the risk of entering the position. I also know that I am always most happy to remain flexible enough to reassess, exit, or even reverse any given position at the point where the market tells me I am better off doing so. And above all this, I know, partially because I have seen it over the years, that I can pick enough successful trades to make it worth my while, and I have found a way to remind myself of this even at the worst of times. Don't get me wrong, I still get stressed some days, especially during early UK market hours, but even when I complain, I am most happy to live with the uncertainty. I still prefer this to any other career or life choice.

To conclude, I am in no way suggesting that you should become me. I am only suggesting that if you do wish to be involved in the financial markets, you should train yourself to learn to accept the uncertainty inherent in it, and react accordingly, leaving your fears aside, and only focusing on making money.

Chapter 15
Staying Flexible

Staying flexible, that is being flexible in your views in trading and investing, is this chapter's topic.

As I wrote in the previous chapter, *"trading and investing is NOT about being always right, it is not even about being fundamentally right but letting this cost you money, it IS just about making money. As follows, in an environment of increased volatility, you have to stay flexible."*

What do I mean by this? I mean that the financial markets, economic conditions, and as follows the price of any financial product you invest in are not static. On the contrary, they are always more prone to change than not. Now this is all great when things are changing in one's favour, but what happens when they don't? Should you just stay there and watch the value of your holdings decrease? Well, in some cases you should, and in other cases you shouldn't. I do not mean to confuse you in any way, so let us try to separate the two cases.

To start with, there are as many trading and investing styles as there are investors and traders. There is no single best one – even though I have come across many that could rightfully be named the worst – nevertheless there is bound to be one that is best suited to your own personality. For this chapter, I shall use my own personality as an example to show you how I try to stay flexible in my own trading, and then hopefully, you can adjust this to your own.

I tend to be a relatively short-term equities trader. I hold on to positions anywhere from a few days to a few weeks. I buy what I believe has a higher fundamental value than its current price, and go short what I believe has a lower one. I have never been a huge fun of technical analysis, but I do always take into account important support/resistance levels as well as daily candlesticks. I do this because even though I do not personally believe in the "magic" of technical formations with exotic names, I do hugely believe in market sentiment, and both the shape of daily candlesticks and the levels where an asset's price has stalled before allow me to understand what other traders and investors are feeling and thinking.

In a practical sense, this means that at the time of writing this chapter (15 November 2015), my portfolios have a number of long CFDs and cash equities positions. These are all holdings in companies that I believe have solid fundamentals and whose valuation according to my fundamental analysis is above the price at which the stocks were bought. However, again at the moment of writing, the European and US Indices have been coming down for a few sessions, and the investing and rest of the world is rather wary of the economic situation in China and greater emerging markets (as well as the recent atrocious terrorist attacks in Paris). So what does staying flexible in this particular situation involve? Does it involve panicking and selling out of all existing positions even at a loss for fear of losing more? Fear can be a very powerful emotion in every aspect of one's life. The problem with it is that it often leads to the wrong decisions. So the answer is no, I for one shall not sell out of all positions based on fear. However, as I have written in the past "arrogance IS a sin", so the fact that the fundamental valuation of certain stocks is above their current market price should in no way make me become blind to their falling prices.

So how have I dealt with this? I have short index positions in the indices these stocks form part of. I also have short positions in individual stocks in certain sectors, at this point, especially the mining one. In addition to these, or perhaps even because I have these in place to protect the monetary value of my long positions (in situations like the current one), I can afford to take a bit more pain seeing my long positions move lower.

I have taken these short positions because over my years of trading, I have learnt that part of being flexible is understanding that there are times when the market as a whole may temporarily move lower, and that when you anticipate this to happen, you should stop just being focused on your fundamental long positions, and instead find a way to protect both the value of these, and move at least to an extent with the market and not against it. I am also happy in situations like this to increase the stops' flexibility I give to my longs, and look to weather the storm.

Now this in no way means that you should give more flexibility to each single trade that starts moving against you and your profits. You most definitely shouldn't. The above described is only a rough roadmap of what you could do in specific overall market circumstances. There are however situations where it is not the overall market that is negative, it is rather a case of the fundamental situation of a specific company whose stock you hold that has changed.

A good example of this is companies issuing profit warnings and cautioning investors that, for example, "they expect no improvement in their financial situation in the foreseeable future." In this case, you are better off biting the bullet and selling out of your position. Yes, at a loss as this unfortunately is not a temporary hiccup, it is, as one of my favourite UK bands once sang, "Grounds for Divorce". And I know how horrible getting out feels when this happens, but things ARE bound to get a lot uglier if you stay. As follows, in this case, staying flexible implies you admitting that what once seemed right (and perhaps at the time even was) IS now wrong, and acting accordingly.

There are, of course, numerous other situations you can come across in your trading and investing that will require you to stay flexible. These two are just examples based on my own experience… and even in my own, this is just the tip of the iceberg, but if nothing else, this chapter will make you think a bit more, and hopefully make you more flexible in your trading and investing.

Chapter 16
New Beginnings

As I write this chapter it is the start of a new year. I like to view each new year as a fresh start, and in fact, I view 2016 as more of one than any other year in my life so far. So for this chapter, I focus on New beginnings. Now for the benefits of this book, we shall only focus on new beginnings in your trading and investing, but... I have always felt that trading and investing are rather real life, in the sense that they always reflect our best and worst personal traits, our psychology, and the current stage of our lives.

Every end of every year is a perfect opportunity to look back, re-assess all investments and trades, learn from our mistakes, and rejoice in our successes. Furthermore, every end is also a new beginning, so we had better enter this new year prepared, clear about our wishes and desires and with a focussed plan on how to achieve them. So let's get down to it. And to do this, do allow me to become less philosophical, and instead be more practical about it all.

We shall start with how to take advantage of the lessons learnt over the last year in order to learn and improve, and then we shall move into how to go about planning for a new year.

1. Assessing Last Year's Investment/Trading Performance

As you may know, there are a thousand and more performance indicators out there. You could use all or none of them, and still be a very successful or, alternatively, a very unsuccessful trader or investor regardless. Personally, I tend to use very few. So here is a list of these, which you may find useful:

- Number of successful vs unsuccessful trades in the last year, as this will help you clearly assess your investment selection process.

- Bigger winners and losers in the last year as this will help you understand if you are using too wide or alternatively too narrow stops, and taking profits too early vs becoming greedy and letting your profits evaporate.

- Overall things you did well or badly trading and investment-wise during the year, and whilst at it, do be honest, but at the same time, do NOT crucify yourself. It is part of human nature to make mistakes, but it is also part of human nature to leave the past behind, and move on being wiser.

- Financial products you used for your trading/investing, and whether these were suitable for your risk appetite, financial situation, knowledge and experience, as well as for the prevailing market environment at the time. This will help you once again gain a clearer understanding of what is and what is not suitable for you, which you can then carry forward to your future investments.

2. Planning for the New Year

As one of my friends wrote and I quote, *"The 1st January 2016 is the first page of a 366 page book. Make it a good one."* And in order to make it a good year I add, you have to fulfil as many of your wishes as you possibly can during it. So the start of the new year is a good time to ask a simple question. What do YOU REALLY want from this year ahead and from the next few years of your life? The possible answers are infinite, and you are the only one that can provide them, but here are some examples to get you thinking.

Do you want capital protection vs capital growth? A steady investment income? A new home? A new job? A family? None of the above? Just money? And are you happy to risk everything to make money? If not, just how much are you willing to risk? On a final note, do you want to make money quickly with no risk? In which case I strongly advise you to stop reading this book for its author does not believe this to be possible so you are wasting your time.

I can also add that what was suitable for you last year may not be suitable moving forward. Your life may have changed or is about to change, or you may wish to change it more yourself. I know I do. So this is something that should always be taken into serious account moving forward.

And finally, very importantly, what has your assessment of your last year in the markets concluded in terms of what you wish to keep or leave behind? You see, I do not know your answers, but I do know mine, so for the benefits of this chapter, I am going to use these as an example. You can adjust these to your own.

Let us start with my risk profile and financial experience, just as most "client knowledge and experience" or to use FCA terms "suitability and appropriateness" questionnaires do. Well, I have been trading and investing for myself and for clients for several years, and I do thoroughly understand most financial products. I have been more than reasonably successful in my trade selection over the last years, so I am confident that this is going to be all right moving forward too. Nevertheless, I am very far from perfect, which means I have made mistakes, and hopefully learnt things in 2015, which I wish to carry with me forward, and on a different level, my own personal wishes and goals have changed over the year, so I need to plan accordingly.

I shall not bore you with all the details of what I learnt from my personal trading and investing last year except to say that on the side of other things, I realized that I may have been best known for being a consistent short-term trader, but I actually perform much better in the medium-term. And as I mentioned earlier, trading and investing is always very "real life", and my own real life and many of my wishes for the future have actually changed this year. You see, on a personal level, I am at a stage of my life where I want to build something that will provide me with stable income, and maybe occasionally capital growth, I do not have my own family yet, but would like to have one one day, I really do not wish to buy a property, and I fully realize that there is no such thing as making money in the markets with no risk attached to it.

So here are some of the specific questions I asked myself which you may find useful:

- How much do I want to risk in the markets in 2016?

- What assets suit my risk profile and financial situation for 2016, for example Equities/Bonds/ETFs/Commodities/Derivatives, etc, and do I have sufficient understanding of these products?

- How much time can I devote to my own personal trading/investing?

- What do I want to get out of it? As in, if I look at the end of 2016, what is that I want to have accomplished through my investing?

- Given all of the above, what is my investment strategy for 2016?

Of course, this list is hardly exhaustive or complete, but I do believe that it will at least make you ask yourself some of the right questions, and if you are honest enough, it will also prompt you to give some really good answers. I do certainly hope it does.

Chapter 17
What Now?

"What now?" many of you asked me back in the beginning of 2016 in the face of what was indisputably the worst start to a year for stock markets in a long time. 2016 saw the worst start for the Dow Jones index in 95 years. So what now Maria, should I sell everything like RBS analysts advised? Should I let the market move lower, then buy because, "It will soon be the right time, just not yet," as Goldman Sachs analysts advised instead? Should I take advantage of current volatility in order to make loads of money, as surely volatility creates a wealth of easy money-making opportunities? The least risk-averse – who I suspect also believe in Santa Claus and the Holy Grail – asked.

You could have done all of the above and be successful or unsuccessful in varying degrees depending on your trading/investing timeframe and exact market entry points, I answered. I do not have your answers, but I do have mine. So for this chapter, I am going to be a bit autobiographical, as I may not know you, but I do know myself, and I believe that I have also learnt to understand the markets, trading/investing and human nature reasonably well by now. (So here goes.)

Financial markets constantly change as they are largely comprised by human beings, and human beings have feelings. They also have beliefs (founded and unfounded), tend to refuse to change and adapt, and often are in denial of objective reality and convinced that if they only find this one perfect trading system, they will become rich overnight. They just have to pick the right night.

Well, Paul Tudor Jones once said that, "In the markets, you have to change and adapt, or die". Now, I started my City career at a proprietary trading desk where some of the world's best traders made huge sums of money by making 100 trades per day each in Fixed

Income and Indices Futures. One day that was over, the markets changed in a way that meant that algorithms could perform this task more efficiently than humans. Those who adapted, lived through that, the rest stopped being in the markets.

I moved into a CFDs trading desk where people were making money by trading stocks and indices using 1-2% stops. That died too, so I left. Then the stock markets turned bullish, and if one was a reasonably good trader, they could make consistent money by buying stocks that had fundamental value, or alternatively selling short stocks that did not, using 5% stops, and trusting that soon enough the stock's price and value would converge, that is that the price would soon revert to the stock's real fundamental value. This time has ended too.

We are currently in an environment where price and value do not converge quickly enough for anyone to make consistent money this way anymore. Why? Because there is too much fear and uncertainty experienced by market participants. Are there fundamental reasons for this? Of course there are. But you can read about these reasons in the Financial Times, Bloomberg, and the rest of the financial press, so I shall spare you from repeating them myself. Instead, I will just describe what I do in this environment.

I still believe in the real fundamental value of certain companies' stocks and in the lack of value of certain others. For example, when I originally wrote this chapter (24 January 2016) in the form of a financial publication article, I still saw value in Royal Dutch Shell shares. At the time of writing this chapter (24 January 2016), RDSA.L shares offered a dividend yield of 9.43%. The Dividend Cover was 2.44, which meant that the company's net income was enough to pay out the total annual dividend announced to all shareholders more than twice. Now I personally believed that even though the price of oil could move lower following my writing this, it would not reach a level where Royal Dutch Shell will stop paying chunky dividends, and go bankrupt. Of course I could have been wrong, but I was most happy to take a view, and buy in.

I also believed in January 2016 that Sainsbury would soon make an offer for Home Retail, and that Ab Inbev were most likely to buy SABMiller, so I was most happy to hold both Home Retail and SABMiller shares. Of course, these deals could have fallen through, and in which case I'd have lost money, but once again, this is a risk I was willing to take.

So, if I am still willing to take risks what has changed in the way I trade/invest? Well, for someone who spent the best part of my career trading short-term, I now have a longer timeframe. I have always believed that both in the markets and in life you should go for things you believe in, and stick with them until or unless proven wrong. This means that in the current market environment, my trading/investing timeframe has moved up from a few days to a few months, years even. My stop loss orders' percentages have also increased. That is if they are there at all, and they are not for cash equities. I trust myself to exit when the market proves me wrong.

Would I still use 2 or 5% stops for any of my trades? No. Why would I? The Average True Range (ATR) of many FTSE 100 and 250 stocks was often routinely above this in the first half of 2016, so why would I hand money to the markets out of plain fear when trading/investing over this time period? I have a view, and until the point when my view changes, what happens intraday has stopped mattering to me. See, I care about value, and I have the time to sit and wait, and the maturity to question myself and exit my bad investments when I ought to. Not when I am scared, not when I hit an arbitrarily chosen x% stop, BUT when I am really fundamentally wrong. And I have accepted that sometimes I will be.

Do I still trade derivatives? Yes, but given my longer timeframe, sometimes I am better off just buying or selling short the actual underlying stocks.

In many ways, all I am saying is, a few days, a few weeks, a few moves the wrong way make no real difference to the real fundamental value of most things in the markets and in life. All you have to do is be selective, be patient, be really honest with yourself, ignore the daily noise, and focus on creating wealth. Not just money, long-term lasting wealth. And yes, there is a huge difference between the two, which we will discuss in the final chapter.

Chapter 18
Building Long-term Wealth with Dividend Income

I finished my last chapter by saying that investors should "Ignore the daily noise and focus on creating wealth. Not just money, but long-term, lasting wealth. And yes, there is a huge difference between the two."

So what really is the difference between money and wealth? I shall attempt to provide you with my own explanation of this by using a metaphor.

As I write, it is 14 February, also widely known as St. Valentine's Day. Before you know it, it has come and gone. You hopefully had fun, overpaid for a fancy four-course meal in an expensive restaurant, exchanged gifts with your loved one, and now you hope that come the same date next year, you will once again be lucky enough to celebrate in a similar fashion. Of course, come the next morning you may realise that you have now spent way more than your personal budget. Even worse, the person you spent it with is not even really the love of your life. I know, ladies and gentlemen, I am unromantic, but bear with me. What I have just described is the real-life equivalent of making money in the short term, and quite likely losing it soon after.

Now let us contrast this to long-term, lasting wealth. Sticking with the same metaphor, let us assume that instead of only celebrating on one specific day each year, you decide that you shall instead love and take care of someone for the long term, whether this is for "as long you both shall live", or as I personally like to interpret it, "for better or worse, and until one of us decides we are better off apart". Together, you will create something valuable that lasts through the years, supports you through your rainy days, and can eventually be passed on to your children. This is long-term, lasting wealth. It is not built in one day, and hopefully once you have it, you are wise enough to not lose it in one day either.

According to the Oxford Dictionary wealth is "An abundance of valuable possessions or money". So how does one create and keep this for the long term when involved in the financial markets? There are many different ways, but for the benefits of this chapter, we shall focus on dividend income.

Now how does one use dividend income to create wealth?

One starts by selecting good quality dividend paying stocks. These are stocks of companies that pay a stable, high dividend compared to the dividend yield of the index of which they are a constituent. (For example, at the time of writing this chapter, the FTSE 100 dividend yield is 4.57%, the S&P 500 dividend yield is 2.37 %.) They should also have a high dividend growth rate (that is the forecast annual growth rate of a company's dividend based on historical dividend payments and dividend predictability), as well as high dividend safety (dividend safety is an indicator expressing the company's ability to continue paying dividends at current or at higher rates in the future).

One then picks a good price level to buy into these stocks. But remember, neither you nor anyone else – regardless of what they might tell you – will ever consistently identify market bottoms, but one should be able to identify price pullbacks, and also clearly identify, based on one's fundamental analysis, when a stock's price is below its current fundamental valuation, and look to take advantage of such opportunities to buy in. However, when one buys for dividend income, one has a much better cushion against market downturns and the perceived need to pick the best possible price. It's then time to sit back and relax; that is, one does not rearrange the dividend portfolio's individual components each week or month, let alone each day. Remember, you bought into these stocks because you believe in the companies' long-term prospects.

However, one should also always stay well informed, be vigilant, and stand ready to get rid of any of the stock holdings should a company decide to cut its future dividends. Don't get me wrong, this may still be a great company, and cutting their dividend may be the best decision their management ever made in order to protect the company's long-term profitability. But income-hungry investors did not sign up for this when they included this share in their dividend income portfolio. Ergo, said stock no longer matches the portfolio's requirements, and ought to be sold.

Last but not least – this is extremely important – when investing in stocks' dividend income, one should make full use of tax-efficient wrappers. By this I mean ISAs and SIPPs. Everyone has an annual allowance, so why not use it? Dividend income is taxable, but is tax free if it is paid within an ISA or SIPP wrapper (please do ask your financial adviser for further details).

Conclusion

I hope that you enjoyed my book, and that it has assisted you in your journey of becoming a better trader. If it has, I will know that you are on your road to success, and I will have fulfilled my promise.

Just remember that just as life is a journey, so is trading and investing. Make it a great one.

Paraphrasing one of my favourite Greek poets, when you do really master trading and investing, you will know you have reached home. It is only at that point that you will truly understand what you whole journey meant.

I AM home.

About the Author

Maria has worked in the City for almost ten years. Having started her career in one of London's biggest proprietary trading desks, Maria then moved into advising high-net-worth individuals on investing and trading equities, bonds, commodities, and derivatives. More recently, Maria moved into wealth management as she wanted to be able to offer a wider range of services to her clients. Currently, Maria works for one of the biggest wealth managers in the UK, a FTSE 100 company, being part of which ensures that she can provide her clients with personally tailored wealth management services designed to meet their individual objectives over the long term. Maria's emphasis always remains on maintaining proactive long-term relationships, and providing her clients with financial security, peace of mind and trust.

Maria holds an MSc in Management from Imperial College London, as well as an MSc in Structural Engineering and a BSc in Civil Engineering from the Aristotle University of Thessaloniki, Greece. In addition to this, Maria holds a number of professional qualifications awarded by the Chartered Institute of Securities and Investments (CISI).

Over the last few years, Maria has been invited to write for several well-known UK financial publications and to discuss her personal views on the financial markets and trading during conferences and on TV.

Maria does not really have much spare time at present, but she plans to spend the time she has in the future travelling the world with her loved ones.

More Books from ADVFN

Super Trading Strategies

by Azeez Mustapha

If you want to be a success trading on the Forex markets, you need to know what you are doing. Learning by trial and error can be expensive and one wrong move could wipe you out. You need help to know what strategies work and how they should be used.

Super Trading Strategies gives you a set of concrete and easy-to-use trading strategies that will help you on your way to making money. They all work on the Forex markets, and some are also applicable to the stock and futures markets.

These super trading strategies include short-term, long-term, swing and positions trading strategies. Some are ideal for part-time traders and some for full-time traders.

Each strategy is explained in detail with examples of how they can be used and charts illustrating the currency movements to which they apply. At the end of each chapter, a strategy snapshot summarises what you have learned.

The strategies were previously published in TRADERS' magazine.

Written by an experienced Forex trader who is also a journalist and writer, *Super Trading Strategies* will help you win the battles of the Forex markets.

Available in paperback and for the Kindle from Amazon.

101 Charts for Trading Success

by Zak Mir

Using insider knowledge to reveal the tricks of the trade, Zak Mir's *101 Charts for Trading Success* explains the most complex set ups in the stock market.

Providing a clear way of predicting price action, charting is a way of making money by delivering high probability percentage trades, whilst removing the need to trawl through company accounts and financial ratios.

Illustrated with easy to understand charts this is the accessible, essential guide on how to read, understand and use charts, to buy and sell stocks. *101 Charts* is a must for all future investment millionaires.

Available in paperback and for the Kindle from Amazon.

The Great Oil Price Fixes and How to Trade Them

by Simon Watkins

The oil market has been manipulated to an extremely high degree for decades, both overtly and covertly, and given its enduring geopolitical importance that is likely to continue.

Traders need to understand the essential dynamics that drive the global oil market, offering as it does unparalleled opportunities to make returns over and above those of other markets. The oil market is also an essential part of trading FX, equities, bonds and other commodities.

This book covers the history of the market, gives you an understanding of the players in the oil game, and provides a solid grounding in the market-specific trading nuances required in this particular field.

Available in paperback and for the Kindle from Amazon.

The Game in Wall Street

by Hoyle and Clem Chambers

As the new century dawned, Wall Street was a game and the stock market was fixed. Ordinary investors were fleeced by big institutions that manipulated the markets to their own advantage and they had no comeback.

The Game in Wall Street shows the ways that the titans of rampant capitalism operated to make money from any source they could control. Their accumulated funds gave the titans enormous power over the market and allowed them to ensure they won the game.

Traders joining the game without knowing the rules are on a road to ruin. It's like gambling without knowing the rules and with no idea of the odds.

The Game in Wall Street sets out in detail exactly how this market manipulation works and shows how to ride the price movements and make a profit.

And guess what? The rules of the game haven't changed since the book was first published in 1898. You can apply the same strategies in your own investing and avoid losing your shirt by gambling against the professionals.

Illustrated with the very first stock charts ever published, the book contains a new preface and a conclusion by stock market guru Clem Chambers which put the text in the context of how Wall Street operates today.

Available in paperback and for the Kindle from Amazon.

For more information on these books and our other titles, go to the ADVFN Books website at www.advfnbooks.com.

ADVFN BOOKS

Printed in Germany
by Amazon Distribution
GmbH, Leipzig